La Salle

—Other titles in the **Great Explorers of the World** series—

COLUMBUS
Opening Up
the New World

ISBN-13: 978-1-59845-101-6
ISBN-10:   1-59845-101-4

MAGELLAN
First to Circle
the Globe

ISBN-13: 978-1-59845-097-2
ISBN-10:   1-59845-097-2

HENRY HUDSON
Discoverer of the Hudson River

ISBN-13: 978-1-59845-123-8
ISBN-10:   1-59845-123-5

MARCO POLO
Amazing Adventures in China

ISBN-13: 978-1-59845-103-0
ISBN-10:   1-59845-103-0

HERNANDO DE SOTO
Spanish Conquistador
in the Americas

ISBN-13: 978-1-59845-104-7
ISBN-10:   1-59845-104-9

VASCO DA GAMA
Discovering the
Sea Route to India

ISBN-13: 978-1-59845-127-6
ISBN-10:   1-59845-127-8

La Salle

Great Explorers
of the World

French Explorer
of the
Mississippi

David Aretha

E **Enslow Publishers, Inc.**
40 Industrial Road
Box 398
Berkeley Heights, NJ 07922
USA

http://www.enslow.com

Library of Congress Cataloging-in-Publication Data

La Salle : French explorer of the Mississippi / David Aretha.
    p. cm. — (Great explorers of the world)
  Includes bibliographical references and index.
  Summary: "Explores the life of René Robert Cavelier, Sieur de La
Salle, from his childhood to his travels to his death, his discoveries
and accomplishments, and his impact on world history"—Provided by
publisher.
  ISBN-13: 978-1-59845-098-9 (hardcover)
  ISBN-10: 1-59845-098-0 (hardcover)
  1. La Salle, Robert Cavelier, sieur de, 1643-1687. 2. La Salle,
Robert Cavelier, sieur de, 1643-1687—Juvenile literature. 3.
Explorers—North America—Biography—Juvenile literature. 4.
Explorers—France—Biography—Juvenile literature. 5. North America—
Discovery and exploration—French—Juvenile literature. 6. Mississippi
River Valley—Discovery and exploration—French—Juvenile literature.
7. Canada—History—To 1763 (New France)—Juvenile literature. I.
Title.
  F1030.5.A74 2009
  977'.01092—dc22
  [B]
                                        2008025054

Printed in the United States of America
012014 Bang Printing, Brainerd, MN
10 9 8 7 6 5 4 3 2

To Our Readers: We have done our best to make sure all Internet Addresses in this book were active and appropriate when we went to press. However, the author and the publisher have no control over and assume no liability for the material available on those Internet sites or on other Web sites they may link to. Any comments or suggestions can be sent by e-mail to comments@enslow.com or to the address on the back cover.

Illustration Credits: Clipart.com, p. 82; Detroit Historical Society, p. 44; Enslow Publishers, Inc., p. 13; The Granger Collection, New York, pp. 3, 10, 38, 48–49, 64–65, 70–71, 74–75, 76–77; Library of Congress, pp. 28, 30, 34, 36; NASA, p. 96; Patricia M. Stafford, pp. 84–85; Ryan Keene, p. 41; © Shutterstock®, pp. 18–19, 54–55, 60–61, 94; Courtesy of the Texas Historical Commission, p. 101.

Ship Illustration Used in Chapter Openers: Library of Congress.

Cover Illustration: The Granger Collection, New York (Portrait of La Salle).

Contents

EXPLORER TIMELINE

1643—*November 22:* René-Robert Cavelier (later known as "La Salle") is born in Rouen, France.

1666—Hungering for adventure, La Salle moves to New France (in present-day Canada) and establishes a prosperous settlement, La Chine.

1669—Launches his first expedition, a multiyear exploration of the St. Lawrence River, Lake Ontario, Lake Erie, and other waters, which may have included the Ohio River.

1673—Contributes to the construction of Fort Frontenac on Lake Ontario.

1674—Travels back to France, where he is named a nobleman.

1676—Oversees the rebuilding of Fort Frontenac, this time in stone.

1678—King Louis XIV approves La Salle's plan to build forts down the Mississippi River.

1679—La Salle launches his second expedition, in which he will sail on the *Griffon*, reach the Illinois River, and build Fort Crevecoeuer.

1680—In his third expedition, La Salle travels to the Mississippi River; he backtracks to find his loyal aide, Tonti, instead of traversing the river.

1682—*February 13:* Launching his fourth expedition, La Salle leads his followers south on the Mississippi River; they soon establish Fort Prudhomme in present-day Tennessee.

April 9: La Salle raises the flag of France at the mouth of the Mississippi, near the Gulf of Mexico; he names the vast territory between the Rocky and Appalachian mountains "Louisiana," and claims it in the name of France.

1683—Speaks with King Louis XIV about establishing a colony and military presence at the mouth of the Mississippi.

1684—*July 24:* Launches his fifth expedition, sailing with three hundred people on four ships to the Gulf of Mexico.

1685—*February:* After sailing well past the Mississippi River, the colonists land at Matagorda Bay in present-day Texas; many of the settlers die due to horrible conditions.

1686—The last of the four ships sinks, leaving the settlers stranded at Matagorda Bay.

1687—*January:* La Salle leads a small party eastward to find the Mississippi River.

March 19: Disgruntled settlers murder La Salle.

Chapter 1

Dreams of Adventure

It was a frigid February morning in Rouen, France, in 1650, and excitement filled the air. Louis XIV, the eleven-year-old king of France, had been touring some of the country's prominent cities with his mother. On this day, he was on his way to Rouen, the capital of Normandy, France. Six-year-old René-Robert Cavelier could not wait to see the boy king.

Robert made his way to Rouen's great square with his parents and his three siblings (little Paul and Marie and older brother Jean). The king's arrival would be very soon, and a great crowd gathered in anticipation. Large bells rang as a gesture of welcome. Paul, Marie, and their mother went to their father's upper-level office to watch the upcoming parade. Robert and Jean joined the crowd on the street, while their father participated in the parade.

Suddenly, the bells stopped ringing and horns sounded in the distance. The king was arriving. The people likely shouted, *"Vive le roi!"* ("Long live the king!"), as was the custom. Robert was awestruck as the royal musicians and the

René-Robert Cavelier, Sieur de La Salle

king's guard, in bright uniforms, marched his way. Then came King Louis himself, riding in a carriage pulled by four horses. Cloaked in fur, the king also wore a hat trimmed with large white plumes. Louis smiled brightly and bowed to the people. His mother followed in a carriage behind him.

After parading through the square, the king came down from his carriage at the city palace. He drew his jeweled sword for all to see and waved it high above his head. The crowd roared in delight. It was a day that few six-year-olds would ever experience—and one that Robert Cavelier would never forget.

Young Robert was a child of privilege. His father was a wealthy merchant. Yet Robert was not content with his status. When he was not in school, he often walked to the banks of the Seine, a river, with Jean or his friends. There they watched sailors unload ships of furs, such as beaver and fox. This special cargo arrived from a land far, far away—from New France in North America.

Robert excelled in mathematics and astronomy at a Jesuit school. But, as one of his teachers claimed, "He is a restless boy."[1] What really fascinated Robert were the adventurers who braved the Atlantic Ocean to journey to New France and explore its new lands and waters. Robert read as much as he could find about such explorations.

11

The elusive and much talked-about—but undiscovered—Northwest Passage to China also intrigued him. He hoped that one day he would be the man to discover the fabled waterway for France and for King Louis.

A TRAILBLAZER IN NEW FRANCE

As Robert grew to adulthood, he came to be known as Sieur de La Salle. *Sieur* means gentleman. Thus, he was referred to as the "gentleman from La Salle." Historians call him by his name and title: René-Robert Cavelier, Sieur de La Salle—or simply La Salle. In both Europe and North America, he is recognized as one of history's greatest explorers.

Had he been born in another era, La Salle might have been lost in obscurity. But in the late 1600s, with much of the Americas unsettled by Europeans, the adventurous Frenchman had the chance to make his mark on history. At the time, European powers ruled various sections of North America. England dominated the colonies along the eastern coast. Spain held vast territory in the southern and western parts of the continent. And France laid claim to land in what is now Canada. This territory was called New France.

Although New France looked impressively vast on a map, the French did not have a strong base

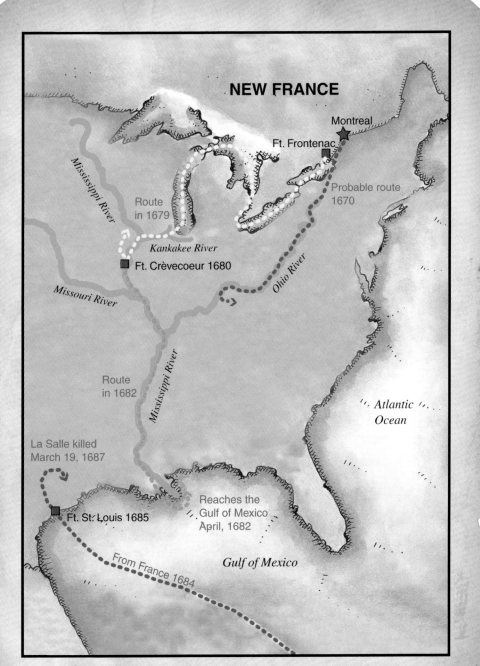

This map shows the routes of all of La Salle's expeditions.

in the region. In 1608, Samuel de Champlain had established the first French colony in the territory, in Quebec. But decades later, only a few thousand French lived in all of New France. Many American Indians lived there, but much of the territory's land, lakes, and rivers had yet to be discovered by Europeans.

When La Salle first sailed to New France in 1666, he burned with desire to explore new territory. He embarked on many grand adventures. La Salle, many believe, was the first European to reach the Ohio River. He explored the Great Lakes like no one had before. And he became the first European to traverse the length of the Mississippi River, from the North all the way to the Gulf of Mexico. Eventually, La Salle would claim the middle third of the current United States for France. He would name this area "Louisiana" in honor of the king who had captured his imagination as a youth in Rouen: Louis XIV.

Unlike previous explorers, La Salle did not seek riches or personal glory. Nor was he, like others, a religious zealot who strove to convert the people he conquered to Christianity. Instead, La Salle pursued adventure for adventure's sake—as well as for the country he loved. Even after his claim of Louisiana, he continued to pursue conquests in the name of France. Time and again, he pushed himself and his followers to go forward in the face of danger. He repeatedly put his life on the line, and he died in pursuit of a quest.

This is the story of a man of grand ambitions who had the courage to go after them—a lifelong dreamer who became a legend. This is the tale of René-Robert Cavelier, the gentleman from La Salle.

Chapter 2

The First Explorations

Born November 22, 1643, René-Robert Cavelier was one lucky baby. France was among the most advanced countries in the world at the time, and his hometown of Rouen was a bustling city. Rouen was just north of Paris and only a few miles south of the English Channel, on the other side of which was England. Rouen was where Joan of Arc had been burned at the stake in 1431. It is also home to the towering Rouen Cathedral, built in 1202, which still stands today.

In the 1600s, ships from other European countries sailed along the English Channel and down the Seine, which flowed past Rouen on its way to Paris. Hundreds of ships each year stopped at Rouen and traded with the city's merchants. With so much business, many of Rouen's traders became very wealthy. Jean Cavelier, Robert's father, was one of the traders.

While Jean conducted business, his wife, Catherine, raised six children—five boys and a girl. Their son Jean was the oldest child, and Robert was the next boy in the family. Robert was an especially

bright child and a favorite of his father. In fact, his father gave Robert the family estate outside the city. This estate was called La Salle, which became Robert's nickname among his family.

GROOMED FOR THE PRIESTHOOD

Jean and Catherine Cavelier were devout Catholics, and they hoped that their boys would grow up to become priests. Jean attended a school

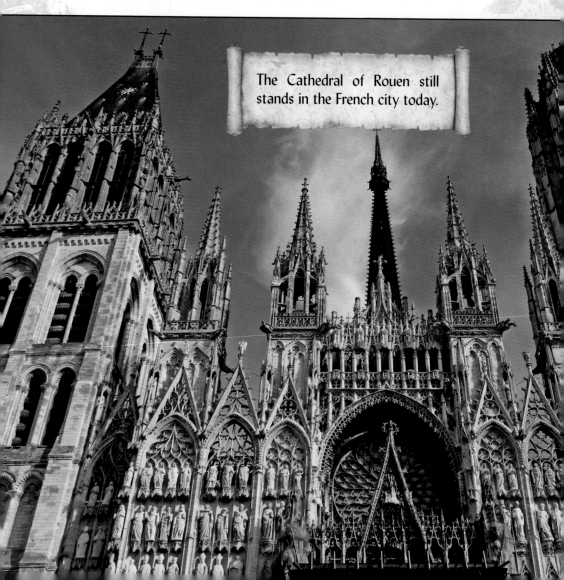

The Cathedral of Rouen still stands in the French city today.

run by Sulpician priests (those belonging to the Society of St. Sulpice in France), while La Salle went to a Jesuit school. Jesuit priests were educated and strict. Robert's day began at 5:00 A.M. He studied mathematics, astronomy, mapmaking, religion, and seven languages: French, Latin, Greek, Hebrew, Spanish, Italian, and Arabic.

At age fourteen, Robert moved to Paris to continue his studies. Two years later, he took the vows of the Jesuit order. This meant that he committed himself to becoming a priest. For the next six years, Robert continued his studies, which included the science of navigation. However, it appears that he was not committed to being a humble servant of God. A superior called him "stubborn, domineering, and hot tempered."[1]

By the mid-1660s, René-Robert Cavelier had become tall and thin with long, curly black hair. At the time, he hoped to become a missionary priest so that he could venture to Asia or other far-off lands. In 1666, La Salle reached a crossroads in his life. His father had recently died, and his brother traveled to New France for missionary work. La Salle asked his superiors if he could be assigned to work in China. The Jesuits denied the request and ordered him to continue his religious studies.

READY FOR A CHANGE

Frustrated, La Salle left the Jesuits. But at age twenty-two, he was not sure what to do with his life. Because the Jesuits had required that he take a vow of poverty, he had not inherited any money from his father. However, his mother and family gave La Salle money so that he could start a new life. He decided that he would follow his older brother to New France. Despite no specific job prospects there, La Salle brimmed with ambition and enthusiasm.

On a chilly March day in 1666, La Salle said goodbye to his mother and siblings. His little nephew, Crevel, bid his uncle a tearful farewell. Peter Saget, a house servant, received permission to go with La Salle. Together they left Rouen for the Atlantic Ocean and the beginning of a brave adventure.

A BRIEF HISTORY OF NEW FRANCE

New France was the territory we know today as eastern and central Canada. In 1666, there was nothing "new" about it. In fact, Frenchman

Jacques Cartier had reached its shores as far back as 1534. Cartier had hoped to find a water passage to Asia. Although he failed to do so, the North American territory seemed promising to him and his countrymen.

More and more French adventurers arrived in New France. They stayed close to the St. Lawrence River, which led from the Atlantic Ocean to the Great Lakes. French settlers traded with American Indians giving them gunpowder, metal, and other inexpensive goods for animal furs, such as beaver. The French then sold the furs to Europeans, who used them to make warm clothing.

More Frenchmen moved to New France in the 1600s. In 1608, Samuel de Champlain established a trading post called Quebec on the St. Lawrence River. He also made alliances with Indian tribes, specifically the Algonquin and Huron. Those Indians allowed French-Catholic missionaries to teach them about Christianity. In 1609, Champlain and his followers helped the Algonquin and Huron fight the Iroquois Indians.

In 1638, Frenchman Jean Nicolet traveled the Great Lakes, hoping to find a water passage west to the Pacific Ocean (and then to China). But the farthest he got was Lake Michigan. Four years later, the French established Montreal on an island in the St. Lawrence River. This is where La Salle's brother, Jean, moved to pursue his missionary work. It also became La Salle's first home when he arrived in New France in 1666.

🌑 LA SALLE'S NEW SETTLEMENT

Moving to Montreal must have been a culture shock for La Salle. The settlement included little more than a church and log cabins that lined a street. Until 1666, the settlers lived in fear of the Iroquois, who had warred with the French for more than twenty years. But that year, French soldiers defeated the Iroquois, who signed a peace treaty with them. Settlers now farmed and traded furs without fear of enemy attacks. La Salle could not have arrived at a better time.

Thanks largely to Jean's influence, the French governor in charge of the territory granted La Salle several thousand acres of forest west of Montreal. The governor hoped La Salle would attract settlers to the region. By doing so, it would better protect Montreal from hostile Indians. La Salle's land, which eventually would be called La Chine, was next to the St. Lawrence River. By traveling west on the river, settlers could find plenty of beaver to kill for their furs.

Although he was not an experienced woodsman, La Salle was productive at La Chine. He kept several hundred acres for himself and rented the rest to fur traders and settlers. These hardy people chopped down trees and built wooden houses.

They hunted deer and moose, whose meat became staples of their diets. La Salle made money not only from renting land but also by trading furs. Within two years, he was wealthy. But, money was not La Salle's primary motivation.

His First Expedition

La Salle, who had learned so many languages back in France, found it helpful to learn Indians' languages as well. The communication helped him trade with Indians. One day, two Seneca Indians sparked La Salle's imagination when they told him about two great rivers. One was the Ohio (which meant "beautiful water") and the other was Missi-Sepe ("big water"), known today as the Mississippi River. La Salle thought that at least one of these rivers might lead to the Pacific and, thus, the riches of Asia. He was anxious to find out.

La Salle traveled to Quebec to tell the governor of New France, Sieur de Courcelles, about his plan. The young adventurer claimed that the expedition would help expand the frontiers of French territory. The French government approved it, but refused to finance it. La Salle would have to pay for the excursion himself. Moreover, it was determined that another party join La Salle's. François Dollier de Casson, a Sulpician priest, would lead a group of missionaries who would try to convert Indians to Christianity.

La Salle was so eager for adventure that he sold all of his property to finance his expedition. He bought four canoes and supplies and hired fourteen men for fifteen months of service. There were also ten missionaries, who had three canoes. In addition, Seneca guides in two canoes would lead the way. On July 6, 1669, the men left La Chine, traveling in canoes southwest on the St. Lawrence River.

The journey was slow and frustrating. Many times fallen trees or large rocks blocked the river. The men had no choice but to haul their canoes and supplies out of the river and carry them. Mosquitoes were a constant nuisance. At night, the men slept along the banks of the river—and hoped it would not rain. For meals, they ate boiled corn, sometimes mixed with fish or meat.

According to some accounts, La Salle lacked good leadership skills. He did not talk much and had few friends. During his expeditions, he pushed his men to continue journeys and punished those who did something unacceptable.

Because he was quiet, many of his men distrusted him. Unfortunately the feeling was mutual. "If I am wanting in expansiveness and show of feeling toward those with whom I associate, it is only through a timidity which is natural to me." Historian Francis Parkman remarked that, "This solitary being, hiding his shyness under a cold reserve, could rouse no enthusiasm in his followers. . . . He trusted himself, and learned more and more to trust no others."[2]

AN UNEASY VISIT WITH THE SENECA

On August 2, the expedition reached Lake Ontario, the most eastern of the five Great Lakes. The men journeyed west along this vast lake, staying close to its southern shore. Although they made good time on the smooth waters, most of them battled some kind of illness. After ten days, they reached Irondequoit Bay—near present-day Rochester, New York—and went ashore. They were about to experience one of the most bizarre periods of their lives.

Seneca Indians greeted the travelers and invited them to their nearby village. The visitors accepted, although La Salle kept some of his men behind to guard the canoes. As gestures of friendship, the two sides offered gifts. The Seneca were happy to receive knives, beads, and other items in exchange for corn, fruit, and pumpkins. They prepared food for their guests: boiled dog meat.

La Salle explained that his men came in peace, and that they were trying to reach the Ohio River. He asked the Seneca if they could offer a guide to the Ohio. They agreed, but the guide would be a captive youth. Moreover, the Frenchmen would

have to wait for the youth to arrive. As it turned out, the explorers waited for more than a week, with still no sign of the young guide. All the while, the Seneca were turning hostile, and La Salle was becoming impatient.

One day, the Seneca invited the explorers to a shocking event. They tied an Indian prisoner to a stake, tortured him for hours, and eventually killed him. Then they boiled parts of his body and ate the flesh. The Frenchmen were appalled and decided to leave as soon as they could.

A CHANCE MEETING WITH JOLLIET

The explorers' stay with the Seneca was not completely fruitless. From them, the explorers learned that they could reach the Ohio River by taking Lake Ontario to Lake Erie and walking south for about four days. The news excited La Salle, and the expedition forged ahead.

When they reached the western end of Lake Ontario, the men heard a persistent roar in the distance. *What could it be?* they wondered. Indians informed them that it came from the Niagara River, which included a huge waterfall and connected Lake Ontario to Lake Erie. Each minute at the Niagara Falls, 4 million cubic feet of water plunged down 170–180 feet in a continuous, thunderous crash. The explorers decided that the

Niagara River was too dangerous to traverse. They walked ahead, carrying their canoes and supplies.

On September 22, they met Algonquin Indians, who seemed friendly. The Algonquin told the travelers that the Ohio River was a six-week journey away, and they offered a Shawnee prisoner to serve as a guide. The explorers were about to continue when they heard that two Frenchman were nearby. One of them was Louis Jolliet, another of North America's greatest pioneers.

Jolliet, like La Salle, had left the priesthood to explore New France. When Jolliet learned from La Salle that the Mississippi River was one of his goals, he told La Salle how to get there: Take the Great Lakes north, all the way up to Lake Superior (above present-day Michigan), and then go west. Jolliet added that the Indians there would benefit from Christianity.

La Salle, however, did not want to travel north to search for the Mississippi when he knew that it lay to the southwest. Moreover, he was not interested in converting Indians. Besides, he said, Jesuit priests already lived and worked in the upper lakes region and would consider the Sulpicians as intruders. Nevertheless, the priests with La Salle wanted to go north. They went north while La Salle and his small group continued west, in search of the Ohio and Mississippi rivers.

Jolliet told the priests traveling with La Salle that the Indians needed lessons in Christianity. Here Jolliet is preaching.

The Sulpicians left in late September, paddling along Lake Erie. They wintered near its shores, and in spring 1670 they took the Detroit River and Lake St. Clair northward. Continuing north, they journeyed up Lake Huron and entered Lake Superior. There, north of present-day Michigan's Upper Peninsula, they reached the Jesuit mission at Sault Sainte Marie. They soon realized that La Salle was right: The Jesuits did not want their help in spreading Christianity. The Sulpicians gave up and went back to Montreal.

LA SALLE REACHES THE OHIO—OR DOES HE?

When the Sulpicians left La Salle's crew in September, Father Galinee went with them—much to the frustration of historians. Galinee had kept a journal of their travels. Once he left, no one remained to chronicle La Salle's subsequent journey through the wilderness. Nineteenth-century historian Francis Parkman claimed that La Salle kept his own journal and later gave it to his niece, but that she lost it in the mid-1700s. Thus, no one is quite sure what La Salle achieved from fall 1669 to 1671.

According to one account, La Salle and his men took the advice of an Indian guide and paddled west along a river. But it turned into marshland, impeding their progress. They then met some

Indians who told them about another river in the distance. La Salle, determined to forge ahead, paddled along the southern waters of Lake Erie. Fifty miles later, he left the lake and walked about twenty miles to Lake Chautauqua. That took him to the Allegheny River, which he took south to the Ohio River.

Some historians believe that La Salle and his crew paddled along the Ohio River in canoes during his first expedition.

Some sources say that La Salle and his crew navigated the Ohio River all the way south to present-day Louisville, Kentucky. At that point, his exhausted crew abandoned him. However, other historians claim that the crew deserted him well before they reached the Ohio River. Still others state that La Salle never reached the Ohio at all, even though La Salle insisted that he had. Historians can only speculate, and it is unlikely that the truth will ever emerge.

PLANS FOR A GREATER EXPEDITION

What seems clear is that La Salle lived in the wilderness from 1669 to 1671 and that he spent a great deal of time on his own. He likely survived on fruit, berries, roots, and the meat of wild game. In 1671, he reappeared in Montreal after what seems like a disastrous expedition. After all, he had spent all his money, he had failed to reach the Pacific, and all his men had abandoned him. Some of his neighbors in Montreal even made fun of him. But La Salle still dreamed of a much grander adventure.

La Salle shared his dreams with Louis de Buade, Count de Frontenac, who recently became the governor of New France. La Salle told Frontenac that, based on his travels and the Indians he had talked to, he knew the whereabouts of a great river that led to the Gulf of Mexico. This river, of course, was the mighty Mississippi. La Salle wanted to launch an expedition to the Mississippi. He and his crew would travel its length, building forts along the way. This would allow France to control the interior of the continent and thus the very profitable fur trade. It would also give La Salle the opportunity for his grand adventure.

Frontenac liked what he heard, but La Salle was not finished. He envisioned a war pitting France and Indians against Spain along the Gulf of Mexico. France would win and take control of the continent from the Appalachian Mountains to the farthest reaches out west. Spain would be confined to Mexico and the Southwest, and the British and Dutch would only maintain colonies east of the Appalachian Mountains.

La Salle's plan might have seemed outlandish, but Frontenac liked the idea of strengthening and expanding New France. In fact, in 1673 he commissioned Louis Jolliet to explore water routes toward Lake Michigan. Accompanied by a priest, Father Jacques Marquette, Jolliet traveled past Lake Michigan and into present-day Wisconsin. While traversing the Wisconsin River, he reached the Mississippi River on June 17, 1673. Frontenac would approve La Salle's trip to the Mississippi— but not quite yet.

⊛ TRUCE WITH THE IROQUOIS

While Jolliet's momentous journey was occurring, Frontenac sent La Salle on an important mission. The governor had heard that the Iroquois Indians were causing trouble in New France. Thus, he sent La Salle to Onondaga (in present-day New York State), capital of the Iroquois confederacy. La Salle invited the Iroquois leaders to a conference near Lake Ontario and the St. Lawrence River.

In early June, Frontenac led four hundred French soldiers and Huron Indians to the big conference. The governor gave gifts to the Iroquois and expressed his sincere desire for peace. Impressed by Frontenac's kindness and perhaps intimidated by his army, the Iroquois signed another peace treaty with the French. As part of the agreement, they allowed the French to build a fort and a trading post near the conference's location. The new establishment would encourage the Indians of the Great Lakes region to trade furs with the French instead of the British. La Salle recommended the site, and workers soon began building Fort Frontenac.

In 1674, Jolliet returned with news of his great discovery. He had traversed the Mississippi River all the way down to where it met the Arkansas River (in present-day Arkansas). He drew maps of his journey, which would prove invaluable.

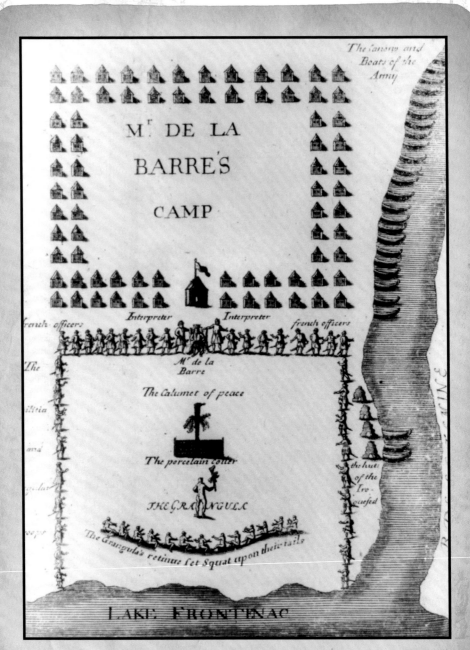

The canoes and Boats of the Army

Mr DE LA BARRE'S CAMP

Interpreter   Interpreter

french officers   french officers

Mr de la Barre

The Calumet of peace

The porcelain cotter

THE GRANGULA

The Grangula's retinue fet Squat upon their tails

the huts of the Iroquois

LAKE FRONTINAC

France and the Iroquois signed a peace treaty. Shown here is the peace meeting between the French and the Iroquois.

La Salle was emboldened by the news. He was anxious to travel the Mississippi all the way to the Gulf of Mexico. But first, he had other issues on his mind.

ELEVATED TO NOBILITY

In 1674, La Salle went to the Palace of Versailles in France. He had two requests for court officials: He wanted to be granted the command of Fort Frontenac, and he wanted to be given the rank of nobility. A letter from Governor Frontenac supported him. La Salle, Frontenac wrote, was "a man of intelligence and ability—more capable of anybody else I know here, to accomplish every kind of enterprise and discovery which may be entrusted to him . . . "[3]

During the winter of 1674–1675, La Salle met King Louis XIV—twenty-five years after seeing the boy king in Rouen. La Salle also befriended an important aide to the king, Jean-Baptiste Colbert. King Louis declared La Salle a nobleman, while Colbert helped La Salle secure the post of governor of Fort Frontenac—albeit with conditions. La Salle had to rebuild the fort in stone, construct a church, and attract settlers to the area. Moreover, he had to pay for all this development himself.

Because of the king's involvement, relatives and friends of La Salle loaned him the money he

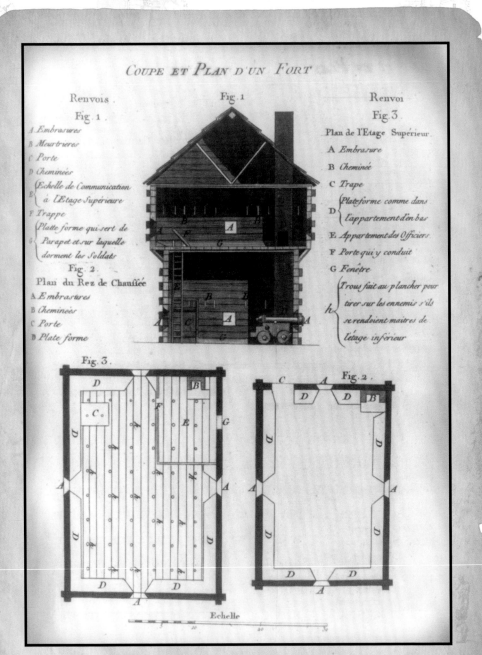

La Salle built trading posts at Fort Frontenac, too. Here is a diagram of a French fort.

needed. He returned to New France and got started on his new enterprise. Over the next two years, La Salle's workers rebuilt Fort Frontenac. It included nine mounted cannons on the stone walls as well as barracks, a mill, and a bakery. La Salle also attracted settlers to farm the land nearby. Moreover, American Indians came in great numbers to trade furs.

La Salle's venture thrived, but his success caused resentment among others. Rival fur traders lost business, while Jesuit priests resented the fact that La Salle allowed priests of a different order in his fort. La Salle's adversaries became so angry with him that they stole furs, defamed La Salle in letters to the king, and tried to turn Iroquois Indians against him. In fact, one of his enemies even tried to kill him.

Nicolas Perrot, who worked at the fort, poisoned La Salle's salad. La Salle became seriously ill and remained so for weeks. Perrot admitted to the assassination attempt, saying he did so on behalf of the Jesuits. La Salle, however, displayed considerable kindness. He absolved the Jesuits and pardoned Perrot.

THE KING APPROVES A MISSISSIPPI VOYAGE

Despite these problems, La Salle was earning a lot of money. "If he had preferred gain to glory," a

Howard Pyle painted this scene, which shows La Salle asking Louis XIV in 1678 for permission to explore the Mississippi.

friend of his wrote, "he had only to stay at his fort, where he was making more than twenty-five thousand livres a year."[4] However, La Salle was not motivated by money. He was determined to fulfill his dream of claiming the Mississippi River territory for France. He sailed back to France to convince the king of his grand plan.

King Louis XIV responded promptly to La Salle's requests. In 1678, he gave La Salle permission in writing to explore the river and establish forts. However, La Salle would have to pay for the venture himself. Once again, La Salle borrowed the money from his wealthy family and friends, promising to pay them back.

While in France, La Salle met a young Italian man with a similar thirst for adventure. Henri de Tonti had served in the French army, and now he wanted to explore North America. Tonti had lost his right hand in a battle, but he replaced it with an iron fist. "Iron Hand," as he was called, proved his physical prowess to La Salle by bashing his metal hand against a wall. La Salle welcomed Tonti as his second-in-command.

For the first part of this expedition, La Salle would use a ship to sail the Great Lakes rather than canoes. He then would take canoes to a major river, which would lead to the Mississippi. Thus, while in France, La Salle assembled blacksmiths and carpenters who later would build the ship in New France. Altogether, he hired thirty men to construct and manage the large vessel. He also bought material to build his ship, including iron, sailcloth, and rope. In July 1678, La Salle, Tonti, and the crew sailed to North America.

NUMEROUS OBSTACLES

Late that summer, La Salle attempted to build the first European ship to ever sail on the Great Lakes. He faced all sorts of problems, one of which was Niagara Falls. Were it not for this impassible obstacle in the Niagara River, La Salle's crew could have constructed the ship on the shores of Lake Ontario, near Fort Frontenac. They then could have sailed along Lake Ontario to the Niagara River to Lake Erie and be on their way. Instead, crew members had to take Lake Ontario to the mouth of the Niagara River, disembark, and walk (with their supplies) past the falls. There they would construct the ship.

But everywhere there was trouble. As crew members built temporary cabins at the construction site, Seneca Indians thought they were trying to take over their land. La Salle appeased them with friendliness and gifts. Later in the autumn, a supply boat carrying the rope, sailcloth, and other vital materials capsized in the Niagara River. All the supplies were lost.

The vast Niagara Falls proved to be an obstacle for La Salle's expedition.

More trouble brewed in Montreal. Those who had loaned La Salle money for his journey now believed the expedition was doomed. La Salle and two others hiked 250 miles in the cold of February from the construction site to Montreal to address the situation. He was met with hostility. Some creditors seized furs that belonged to La Salle. Others demanded that they be awarded Fort Frontenac as compensation. La Salle could not solve this financial mess. He and his men acquired as many supplies as they could and journeyed back to the construction site.

SAILING THE GRIFFON

La Salle's fortunes had improved by the summer of 1679, when the crew completed building the ship. They called it the *Griffon* after a mythical bird that is part eagle and part lion—both fast and powerful. On August 7, the crew raised *Griffon*'s sails. About thirty men prepared to begin the great adventure. Joining them was Father Louis Hennepin, invited by La Salle to provide spiritual strength.

Spirits ran high as the ship made good time crossing Lake Erie. (It was much easier than paddling in canoes.) After resting and replenishing supplies near present-day Detroit, they sailed north on Lake Huron. Powerful rain and wind, raging for hours, pounded the ship, but the crew managed to weather the storm. Eventually, the *Griffon* reached the northern end of Lake Huron, near the northern tip of present-day Michigan's Lower Peninsula. From there, Lake Superior lay to the north and Lake Michigan to the west.

The crew stopped at a community called Mackinac, where Jesuit priests, French fur traders, and Ottawa Indians lived. Before their expedition began, La Salle had sent fifteen scouts in canoes to Mackinac to lavish gifts upon the Ottawa. When La Salle arrived upon the *Griffon*, he found that the men had betrayed him. They traded the "gifts" to the Indians for furs and wine and left the scene.

La Salle ordered Tonti to search for the scouts. Meanwhile, he and his crew sailed west to Lake Michigan, all the way to an island in Green Bay. Remarkably, some of the French deserters actually were on the island—with an enormous amount of furs.

La Salle then made a pivotal decision. He would have some of his crew return the *Griffon* back to the Niagara River, for two reasons. First, he knew of no river that connected Lake Michigan to the Mississippi, and the *Griffon* could not be hauled over land. Second, the crew could sell the furs and use the money to pay back some of La Salle's creditors.

So, on September 18, 1679, fourteen men took the *Griffon* back to its starting point. The rest,

LED by LA SALLE DISCOVER

This stained-glass window called "City of Detroit III" depicts La Salle (left) and a priest landing on the shore of what would become Detroit.

including La Salle, traveled via canoes to the southeast end of Lake Michigan where great trouble awaited.

NEAR~DEATH EXPERIENCES

Weather was the first great danger. Storms capsized the canoes multiple times. All of the crew's supplies were lost. The men relied on the savvy hunting skills of their Shawnee guide, Nika, for food. By November 1, they reached their destination: the point where the St. Joseph River (in present-day southern Michigan) meets Lake Michigan. Tonti and twenty others, traveling overland from Mackinac, were supposed to meet La Salle, but they had yet to arrive. Tonti and ten men finally arrived three weeks later. They brought supplies, but they also reported that the *Griffon* had disappeared.

In early December, La Salle led a group of thirty-three men up the St. Joseph in search of a river that would lead to the Mississippi. It certainly was not a wise decision to be exploring in December, as La Salle soon found out. One day, while the men were ashore, La Salle entered the woods searching for the river. Heavy snow began to fall, and he became lost in the whiteout. By nightfall, he still could not find his way back to camp. He did spot a small bonfire, which no one was using, and warmed himself next to it throughout the night. In the morning, he spotted fresh footprints in the snow next to where he slept. La Salle realized that he had "stolen" an Indian's fire—and felt fortunate he had not been killed.

La Salle found his companions the next day, and soon Nika led them on a hike to the Kankakee River. But during the trek, La Salle was nearly killed again—by one of his own men. A French-man named Duplessis, like many others before and after, hated La Salle for pushing him too hard. He pointed a gun at La Salle's back and fired. Only the heroics of another man, who swatted the gun just before the would-be assassin pulled the trigger, saved him from being shot. Surprisingly, La Salle did not punish Duplessis.

The men soon reached a stream, which they took to the long-awaited Kankakee River. Despite the winter weather, they canoed along the Kankakee to the Illinois River. This waterway cuts through the present state of Illinois and leads to the river they so badly sought: the Mississippi. But this group of explorers would not reach their goal. A series of disasters awaited them.

HEARTBREAKING NEWS

In January 1680, the men stopped in present-day Peoria, Illinois, home to a large village of Illinois Indians. The Indians stormed toward the shore with weapons, startling the visitors. But La Salle insisted that he and his men came in peace. Although the Illinois offered them food and shelter, the Indians were not to be entirely trusted. The Indians turned surly when they heard, falsely, that the French visitors were allies of the Iroquois, the Illinois's rival. One Indian even poisoned La Salle's food. He was saved, according to Tonti, by medicine brought from France.

Sensing trouble, six of the explorers deserted. La Salle decided to make camp nearby for the winter, but he kept his men busy. First, they constructed Fort Crevecoeur (French for "brokenhearted"). He also assigned one group to build a new ship, which he planned to sail down the Illinois and Mississippi rivers. Another party scouted the Illinois River to find the Mississippi.

As for La Salle, he, Nika, and four others journeyed overland toward home to Montreal, more than a thousand miles away. The trip took about two months. They battled ice and snow, waded through frigid water, struggled to find food, and had to avoid warring Iroquois.

When he finally arrived in Montreal in May 1680, La Salle discovered that he had lost most of his property. He gathered supplies for his forts, but that summer he received devastating news: Deserters had destroyed the three forts he had built since 1678—the ones on the Niagara and

Although La Salle's party feasted in the Illinois village in 1680, the Europeans did not completely trust the Illinois people. George Catlin painted this scene in 1847.

St. Joseph rivers as well as Fort Crevecoeur. More frightening, they were on their way to murder La Salle. The French nobleman, however, outwitted his enemies. When they arrived on the shores of Lake Ontario, soldiers led by La Salle captured the group and arrested them.

After more than a decade of financing his own expeditions, La Salle was practically broke. His long winter treks had been excruciating. The forts he had built, as well as the *Griffon*, were gone. On at least four occasions, people had tried to kill him. And yet his spirit remained unbroken. Robert Cavelier, Sieur de La Salle, was determined to conquer the Mississippi.

Chapter 3

Down the Mighty Mississippi

In August 1680, La Salle launched his third voyage to the west. He and two dozen men were off to Fort Crevecoeur, where they would finish building the ship that would sail the Mississippi. Again, La Salle's crew traveled the Great Lakes to the Illinois River. Some of the men were left at Mackinac and others departed at the St. Joseph River settlement. For La Salle and the small crew that remained, horror awaited them on the Illinois River.

When the men first spotted the Illinois Indians' community, they knew something was terribly wrong. The entire settlement had been burned to the ground. Corpses of the Illinois littered the ground. The bodies of dead women and children were tied to stakes. La Salle knew this had been the ghastly work of the Iroquois. He feared that Tonti might be among the dead, although no one found any trace of him.

Fort Crevecoeur, the crew confirmed, had also been torn down. But La Salle mostly worried about Tonti and his followers. La Salle and his crew traveled southwest on the Illinois River looking for the lost men. They journeyed all the way to the Mississippi. Many of the men suggested that they begin their exploration of the Mississippi River right then and there. Weather conditions were favorable; since it was December, it made sense to continue south. But La Salle insisted they keep searching for his loyal lieutenant, Tonti.

● BRIGHTER DAYS AHEAD

In the dead of winter, the crew journeyed to Fort Miami, where the St. Joseph River meets Lake Michigan. The trek was arduous, with exceptionally cold weather and snow that rose to the men's waists.

In the early months of 1681, La Salle tended to a brewing crisis: the Miami and Illinois tribes were at odds with each other. Unless the two tribes allied together, La Salle believed, the Iroquois would take advantage of the situation and try to take over the region. With the Great Lakes area in chaos, he feared, the British might capture the territory. Such a scenario would threaten French occupation. La Salle convinced the Miami and Illinois that they would be better off as allies than foes. At a grand council, the two groups agreed to peace—with themselves and with the French.

It seemed La Salle's luck was changing. That spring, he learned the joyous news that Tonti was alive, living with Pottawatomie Indians near Mackinac. On May 25, 1681, La Salle paddled north to Mackinac to greet his longtime friend, as well as Father Zenobe Membre. Together, they returned to Montreal.

La Salle, his companions learned, was still determined to pursue his dream. Membre, like so many others, was amazed at the man's resiliency:

> Anyone else would have thrown up his hand and abandoned the enterprise; but, far from this, with a firmness and constancy, that never had its equal, I saw him [La Salle] more resolved than ever to continue his work and push forward his discovery.[1]

OFF TO THE MISSISSIPPI

In Montreal, La Salle met with Governor Frontenac, the leader of New France. Despite his failed expeditions in the past, La Salle had fresh ideas about exploring the Mississippi River. He would only travel with canoes, and Indians as well as Frenchmen would go with him. La Salle raised money for his fourth western expedition.

In September 1681, La Salle, twenty-three Frenchmen, and thirty-one Indians began their journey. La Salle was glad to travel with his top aide, Tonti, as well as his skilled Indian guide, Nika. Traveling the familiar route, some of the canoes reached the Mississippi on February 6, 1682. Others traveling at a slower pace eventually caught up.

When he began to travel down the Mississippi River, La Salle realized just how wide the body of water could be.

La Salle planned to establish small settlements along the Mississippi, all the way down to the Gulf of Mexico. Eventually, France would secure the gulf area as well, ousting the Spanish. Then, France would control all of the Great Lakes region, the territory north of it, and the vast interior of the continent. First, however, La Salle would try to become the first European to travel the length of the Mississippi. On February 13, the momentous voyage began.

In Honor of Pierre Prudhomme

The Mississippi River got its name from the Chippewa Indians. In their language, *Mississippi* means "large river." But in La Salle's mind, the river now became the property of France. He named the river "Fleuve Colbert" after an old acquaintance: Jean-Baptiste Colbert, minister to King Louis XIV.

Tonti kept a memoir of the voyage, but he did not record the expedition's experience with the Missouri River. The water from that large river rushes into the Mississippi, which undoubtedly made for perilous travel. After the Missouri, the Mississippi flowed smoothly and the days became warmer. Fields and forests lined the river, and it seemed uninhabited on both sides.

In late February, south of the Ohio River in present-day Tennessee, the crew set up camp along the shore. They did not expect to stay long until one of the men, an armorer named Pierre Prudhomme, got lost in the woods while hunting. La Salle feared that Indians had killed Prudhomme, yet he did not want to leave without knowing his whereabouts. While some of the crew searched for Prudhomme, others constructed a small fort to protect them from possible Indian attacks. After six days, an exhausted Prudhomme finally returned. La Salle was so pleased, he named the new construction Fort Prudhomme.

WELCOMED BY THE QUAPAW

In mid-March, the explorers approached the Arkansas River. This is the point that French explorers Louis Jolliet and Jacques Marquette had reached in 1673 before turning back. Around this area, La Salle's crew encountered a thick fog. From the shore, they heard the cries of American Indians and the pounding of drums. Concerned that the Indians might be hostile—and unable to see them—the crew landed on the opposite shore and began to build a fort.

When the fog cleared, however, the Indians paddled across the river to meet the strange guests. La Salle offered a peace pipe to these Quapaw Indians, who turned out to be exceptionally

kind and welcoming. Father Membre wrote that they were moved by his religious ceremony: "During this time they showed that they relished what I said by raising their eyes to heaven, and kneeling as if to adore."[2]

At one point, the French guests attached the coat of arms of the French king to a wooden cross. La Salle declared possession of the land for France, and his people cried, "Long live the king!" After three days with the Quapaw, the explorers continued down the Mississippi.

ALLIGATORS AND THE SMELL OF DEATH

It was now late March, and the crew enjoyed the warm pleasures of springtime in the South. They saw alligators for the first time and killed them for food. They also came across more American Indian villages. As with the Quapaw, La Salle made friends easily and then declared their territory a possession of France. The Indians did not understand the ways of the Europeans, and as a result often lost their rights to their land without realizing it.

At one point while traveling down river, Indian guides who had joined the expedition noted that a large lake lay next to the Mississippi. Beyond that lake was the impressive community of the Taensa Indians. Curious, La Salle sent Tonti and other

members of his group to explore. They were amazed to see a city of houses, made of brick and mud. These homes even had roofs, built from cane and straw. Again, relations were friendly. The Taensa chief accompanied Tonti back to camp, where La Salle offered him gifts. Later, the crew landed near the present-day city of Natchez, Mississippi. As before, they planted a French coat of arms.

Despite their peaceful encounters so far, La Salle worried about coming across Spaniards, who would resent their intrusion. As it turned out, encounters with two Indian groups in the Deep South brought more immediate danger. One group of Indians greeted the explorers' presence with a volley of barbed arrows. The crew contin-ued on, but after just a few miles downriver, they encountered the razed village of Tangipahoa. Enemies had massacred the Indians of the village. To La Salle and his men, this was a sobering reminder of the dangers of their journey. Fortu-nately, they were approaching their ultimate destination.

● La Salle Claims Louisiana

On April 6, 1682, the crew reached a point on the Mississippi where the river branched into three channels. La Salle split up his expedition and ordered groups to explore the different branches

La Salle and his men ate the alligators that lurked in the muddy Mississippi River.

of the river. Soon after leading his group down one channel, La Salle realized he was approaching the Gulf of Mexico. The water tasted salty, like seawater, and the river opened to a seemingly endless body of water.

After a twenty-five-hundred-mile journey, it was time to celebrate. La Salle had reached his destination. He thus became the first European explorer to travel the Mississippi from the North to its southern most point.

The three parties soon joined together. On April 8, they made camp on the shore of the western channel. The next day, they assembled on an elevated knoll. The crew erected a large pillar and painted the arms of France on it. Also on the pillar, they wrote the words: "Louis the Great, King of France and Navarre, reigns the 9th of April, 1682."[3] Men fired their muskets, cried "Long live the King,"[4] and sang in celebration.

Beneath the pillar, they placed a plaque that read: "Robert Cavelier, with Lord Tonti—ambassador, Zenobio Membré—Recollét, and twenty Frenchmen, first navigated this river from the country of the Illinois, and passed through this mouth on the ninth of April, sixteen hundred and eighty-two."[5]

La Salle declared that France now possessed the territory on both sides of the Mississippi. He named this territory Louisiana in honor of his king, Louis XIV. Louisiana included all the land east of the Rocky Mountains and west of the Appalachian Mountains. This territory was approximately the middle third of the present United States.

La Salle proclaimed:

> [I take] possession in the name of His Majesty and successors of his crown, of this country of Louisiana, seas, harbors, ports, bays, adjacent straits and all its nations, peoples, provinces, cities, boroughs, villages, mines, ore-bearing earth, fishing waters, salt-water rivers, rivers, included in the extent of the said Louisiana.[6]

After a religious ceremony and the planting of a large cross, the historic event concluded. La Salle had just claimed an area that was larger than France itself. His work on this expedition was done. It was time to go home.

LA SALLE'S NEW ENEMY

Heading north on the Mississippi, the explorers struggled to find food. At first, they killed alligators for meat, but those big reptiles became harder to find as the crew journeyed north. They traded goods for corn with the Quinipissas Indians, but this was the same tribe that had attacked them with arrows days earlier. At night, the Indians attacked the explorers' camp. La Salle's party kept them at bay with gunfire, then left the area.

La Salle claims Louisiana for France on April 9, 1682, in this George Catlin painting.

For La Salle, the next few months would be disastrous. After stopping at Fort Prudhomme, he became ill from disease, possibly malaria. For more than a month, he and his followers worried that he might die. Although he gradually recovered, he would remain weak for months afterward. All the while, Tonti and others continued on to Mackinac. They planned to pass the news of their discovery to Governor Frontenac, but they were unaware of the turmoil brewing back home.

Unhappy with Frontenac, King Louis XIV replaced him with a former naval officer named Le Febvre de la Barre. The king instructed La Barre to concentrate on cultivating the land of New France and forget about western expansion. However, the king stated, La Salle's explorations were acceptable because he seemed to be accomplishing a great deal.

But right from the beginning, La Barre had it in for La Salle. He sided with the Jesuits of New France, who resented La Salle's alliance with Franciscan priests. La Barre sent letters to Jean-Baptiste Colbert, minister to the king, stating that La Salle did not reach the gulf and that he neglected Fort Frontenac. He also claimed that La Salle had upset the Iroquois, who now posed a threat to French trade in the West. Believing La Barre's lies, the king wrote that "the discovery of the Sieur de la Salle is very useless, and that such enterprises ought to be prevented in future."[7]

Thinking the king was now on his side, La Barre confiscated Fort Frontenac and all of La Salle's property. He also ordered soldiers to capture La Salle's supply stations at Niagara and Mackinac and his forts on the Illinois River. By September 1682, La Salle was unaware of this mission—although he did know that La Barre was in charge and had it in for him.

That fall, La Salle hoped to strengthen his position on the Illinois River. Thus, he decided to establish a colony where Fort Crevecoeur had been. Through the spring of 1683, he oversaw the construction of a fortress atop a high bluff. He called it Fort St. Louis. Before its completion, La Salle learned of La Barre's quest to destroy his forts and settlements. Yet La Barre's plans were even more sinister. In discussions with the Iroquois, he gave them approval to plunder Fort St. Louis and kill La Salle.

A Meeting With the King

At this point, La Salle had no choice but to speak with the king. In the fall of 1683, he sailed back to France for a meeting with the king. Louis liked La Salle and realized that La Barre's disparaging remarks about him were lies. The king ordered

La Barre to return all of La Salle's belongings. He also named La Salle commander of the territory from the Illinois River down to Mexico.

Moreover, the king learned from La Salle that the Spanish seemed to have a weak hold on the Gulf of Mexico. In fact, La Salle reported that he had not seen any Spaniards around the mouth of the Mississippi. Hearing this, King Louis decided it would be wise to establish a French colony right at the mouth of the river. It would give France control of the Mississippi from the bottom to the top. The king wanted La Salle to form an alliance with Indians in preparation for an attack on the Spanish. Not one to disappoint his king, La Salle prepared for his fifth major expedition.

A Voyage of Misery

On July 24, 1684, La Salle launched his largest expedition yet, made up of some three hundred people. A hundred French soldiers—as well as laborers, women, and children—set sail on four ships. They would travel from France to the Gulf of Mexico. La Salle's brother, Jean, and his nephew, Crevel de Moranget, joined them. The voyagers even took livestock, such as cows and chickens, to breed at their destination. They planned to establish a colony in the gulf near the mouth of the Mississippi.

Soon after the ships left port, they had to return because the warship *Joly* needed repairs. La Salle's "soldiers" were actually the dregs of society, including criminals and pirates. (Men who manned ships on such journeys often came from the lower rungs of society, or even from prison.)

During the voyage, many people became sick, and some died. La Salle himself suffered from a dangerously high fever. Moreover, he quarreled with Captain Beaujeu, the commander of the fleet. Beaujeu, in a letter to his friend, wrote of La Salle: "Don't you know that this man is impenetrable, and that there is no knowing what he thinks of one? . . . His distrust is incredible. If he sees one of his people speak to the rest, he suspects something, and is gruff with them."[8]

The troubles only worsened. Spanish pirates captured the supply ship *St. François*, which included food and building supplies. When the Frenchmen reached the colonized island of Hispaniola (located between Cuba and Haiti), La Salle was still very sick. While he convalesced for two months on the island, some of his fellow crew members were killed in fights or contracted diseases. By November, La Salle recovered enough to continue the journey.

Spaniards learned about the French voyage and sent warships to the Gulf of Mexico. Beaujeu's fleet luckily avoided the enemy vessels, but they could not find the mouth of the Mississippi. The maps that La Salle referred to were wrong. They passed the mouth of the Mississippi but did not realize it. For days, they kept on sailing west, looking for a destination that they had already passed. Beaujeu was furious. On January 6, 1685, La Salle decided to find a place to go ashore. Too many crew members were sick. Supplies had greatly diminished. They could not go on.

DESPERATION AND DEATH AT FORT ST. LOUIS

The ships dropped anchor in Matagorda Bay in present-day Texas. However, one of the vessels ran aground and was destroyed—its food and supplies lost for good. They were down to two ships. La Salle asked Beaujeu to explore the coast with the *Joly* to search for the Mississippi. However, the disgruntled captain kept heading east—all the way back to France. Now La Salle and his men just had one ship.

The rest of La Salle's group went ashore on February 20. About 150 settlers tried to survive near Matagorda Bay. La Salle oversaw the

After missing the mouth of the Mississippi River, La Salle's ships landed on the coast of present-day Texas in 1685.

cl. et fec

construction of a fortress, which he called Fort St. Louis. But because of the lack of trees and good carpenters, the fort was less than impressive. Over time, the number of settlers gradually dwindled. In the hot climate, they struggled to grow crops. Many died from disease, snakebites, and poisonous plants. Others wandered off, never to be seen again. After the last of the ships was wrecked while exploring the coast, the settlers felt completely deserted. Only about three dozen settlers remained, and many of them blamed La Salle for their predicament.

In January 1687, after two grim years at Matagorda Bay, La Salle took action. He and twenty other males (including Jean, Moranget, and Nika) trekked eastward on foot to find the Mississippi. If they did, they would paddle northward to one of the French forts that La Salle and Tonti had founded. But after walking for two months on sometimes swampy terrain, the men still did not find the Mississippi.

By this point, the men were exhausted and in ill health. Some were furious with La Salle, whom they felt was leading them on another useless journey. Much like his many previous followers, they also felt that he pushed them too hard. Some did not like Moranget, either, considering him rude and abrasive. The men made camp near the Trinity River in Texas on March 15.

MURDER IN THE WILDERNESS

While at camp, La Salle sent Nika and a half-dozen other men to find food. After Nika killed two buffalo, the men sent a message to La Salle, asking for help carrying the carcasses back to camp. La Salle sent his nephew Moranget and some horses (which had carried supplies for the men throughout the journey). When Moranget found the site, he saw one of them, Duhaut, smoking the meat in order to preserve it. Duhaut and three others also had set aside the best portions of the meat for themselves, which angered Moranget. La Salle's nephew took the meat away and told them they would not get any of it.

Duhaut and four other men—Liotot, Hiens, Teissier, and L'Archevêque—had reached their boiling point. Together they conspired to kill Moranget as well as two of La Salle's faithful followers—Nika and Saget. At the site of the buffalo kill, the conspirators waited until the three men fell asleep. Liotot, a surgeon by trade, killed Moranget with axe blows to the head. He did the same to Nika and Saget.

The killers agreed that La Salle would be their next target. However, the river back to camp was temporarily impassible because it had risen due to recent heavy rainfall. The men stayed put, but

73

La Salle visited the Caddo Indians in May 1686. George Catlin painted this historic scene.

La Salle—worried about his nephew's safety—headed to the conspirators' camp. On March 19, he arrived there along with Father Anatase Douay. When La Salle asked about Moranget's whereabouts, L'Archevêque replied that he was wandering around somewhere.

Just moments later, Duhaut and L'Archevêque pulled their guns and fired at La Salle. Duhaut's shot struck La Salle in the head, killing him. Father Douay witnessed the fatal shot, and now worried about his own life. But the conspirators on that day cared only about killing La Salle, who they felt had caused them more than two years of torment. The men cursed him and tore off all of his clothes. They blamed him solely for their dire situation.

Sieur de La Salle, one of the most renowned explorers in French history, never received a formal burial. Instead, his killers dragged his body to the bushes and left him there naked, for wild animals to devour.

La Salle was murdered by one of his own men in 1687.

Henri Joutel, a soldier who traveled on La Salle's final expedition, summarized the life and death of the French explorer:

> He had a capacity and talent to make his enterprise successful; his constancy and courage and extraordinary knowledge in arts and sciences, which render him fit for anything, together with an indefatigable body, which made him surmount all difficulties, would have procured a glorious issue to his undertaking, had not all those excellent qualities been counterbalanced by too haughty a behavior, which sometimes made him insupportable, and by a rigidness to those under his command, which at last drew on him an implacable hatred, and was the occasion of his death.[9]

THE FATE OF HIS FOLLOWERS

Though La Salle had died, his quest to reach the Mississippi remained alive. His brother, Jean Cavelier, and others actually made it to the great river. They paddled north and eventually found Tonti, who was working at Fort Prudhomme. While heartbroken by the death of La Salle, Tonti helped Jean and the others return to France. They were the lucky ones.

Back at Fort St. Louis, near Matagorda Bay, the colonists continued to suffer and die. "They were . . . racked by disease, threatened by hostile Indians, assailed by mosquitoes and lots of deadly snakes," said Don Chipman, history professor at the University of North Texas. "Just terrible, terrible conditions under which to live."[10]

In January 1688, Karankawas Indians attacked the remaining settlers still alive at Fort St. Louis. They killed everyone except six children, whom the Indian women raised for years until turning them over to the Spanish. In 1689, Tonti sent out search missions to the Matagorda Bay area, but they failed to find any survivors. In 1721, a Spanish fort replaced Fort St. Louis, officially ending La Salle's settlement in present-day Texas.

Chapter 4

La Salle's Historical Importance

As a child in France in the 1650s, La Salle was one of many boys who dreamed of exploring the New World. But he also had the qualities needed to achieve his ambitions. Certainly, he was blessed with wealth and education. But what set him apart was his relentless determination. He persevered time and time again, often overcoming seemingly impossible odds.

In untamed wilderness, he walked for weeks on end. Through brutally cold winters, he pressed forth with conviction. When encountering American Indians, he was able to befriend them and establish peaceful relationships. He lived on whatever the earth offered, from nuts and berries to buffalo and alligator. He overcame financial ruin and the destruction of his boats and forts. He twice bounced back from life-threatening illnesses, and he escaped assassination attempts on several occasions.

La Salle, a quiet man who kept his thoughts to himself, created many enemies. His creditors fretted about their money. Those in power resented his accomplishments. The men on his expeditions said

La Salle went down in history as a great explorer of North America.

he pushed them too hard. But to La Salle, money, politics, and hurt feelings mattered little. His life had a greater purpose—to explore new worlds no matter the hardship, to expand the empire of France for his beloved king, Louis XIV.

TRAILBLAZER AND CONQUEROR

When La Salle first arrived in New France in 1666, few of his countrymen populated the territory. A census taken that very same year (the first ever conducted in North America) revealed that only 3,215 French men and women lived in the colony. Like many other western European countries—including Spain, England, Holland, and Portugal—France wanted to expand and strengthen its global empire. Among Frenchmen in North America, no one furthered that goal more than La Salle.

First he built a settlement at La Chine, expanding French territory west of Montreal. He also played major roles in the establishment of Fort Frontenac near the St. Lawrence River and Lake Ontario. This strategically located outpost helped the French dominate the fur trade in the region (to the frustration of the British).

During his expeditions, La Salle broke new ground. He was the first European to traverse the Great Lakes by ship. His discovery (or alleged discovery) of the Ohio River helped the French

establish a presence in the region. Decades later in 1753, George Washington on behalf of the colony of Virginia asked Gardeur de St. Pierre why the French had built a fort on the nearby Monongahela River. St. Pierre, the commandant at Quebec, responded: "We claim the country on

La Salle was the first European to cross the Great Lakes by ship. The first of the lakes that the *Griffon* crossed was Lake Erie.

the Ohio by virtue of the discoveries of La Salle, and will not give it up to the English. Our orders are to make prisoners of every Englishman found trading in the Ohio Valley."[1] George Washington and his force retreated, leaving the French in control at the time. Certainly,

La Salle's many discoveries altered the course of American history.

Many times, La Salle made friends with American Indian groups. He brought the Miami and the Illinois Indians together in 1681, which kept the peace in the lower Great Lakes region. Throughout his journeys, La Salle staked out territory under the flag of France. He constructed forts along the Niagara River, the St. Joseph River (Fort Miami), the Illinois River (Fort Crevecoeur), the Mississippi (Fort Prudhomme), and in Texas (Fort St. Louis).

In his first three expeditions, La Salle explored the Great Lakes as well as major rivers in the present-day Midwest. In his fourth journey, he proved that one could travel by water from Montreal all the way to the Gulf of Mexico. En route, he became the first European explorer to traverse the Mississippi to its southern end.

According to international agreements at the time, the country that occupied the mouth of a river had the right to claim all the territory through which that river flowed. This included any land drained by its tributaries. Thus, when La Salle reached the mouth of the Mississippi at the Gulf of Mexico, planting his pillar and cross, he claimed for France all of the Mississippi's adjacent territory.

Louisiana, as he called it, was much vaster than the boot-shaped southern state that bears its name today. The massive region comprised 820,000 square miles. La Salle's conquest gave New France territory from Hudson Bay in present-day Canada south to the Gulf of Mexico. From east to west, the land stretched from the Appalachian Mountains to the Rocky Mountains.

EIGHTY YEARS OF FRENCH RULE

Louisiana boasted the best farmlands in North America. After La Salle claimed Louisiana in 1682, France controlled the territory for a full eighty years. In 1699, Pierre Le Moyne d'Iberville started the first permanent settlement in French Louisiana. Called Biloxi, it was established in present-day Mississippi along the Gulf of Mexico. Antoine Laumet de La Mothe founded Detroit in 1701. A year later, Mobile took root in present-day Alabama.

In 1716, Frenchman Jean-Baptiste Le Moyne, Sieur de Bienville, finished constructing Fort Rosalie on the Mississippi in present-day Natchez, Mississippi. Two years later, Bienville established a settlement at New Orleans. This critical port city on the Gulf of Mexico was the gateway to the Mississippi River. Whichever country held New Orleans could control the American heartland. France hung on to New Orleans until the 1760s.

During that period, a strong French culture was established there that has survived into the twenty-first century.

In 1763, France lost the Seven Years' War, which in colonial America was called the French and Indian War. As such, it was forced to cede the eastern section of Louisiana to Britain; it ceded the western region to Spain to keep it from Britain. But the French still made their presence felt. In 1764, Pierre Laclède founded St. Louis on the western side of the Mississippi River. This city would become known as the "Gateway to the West." From there in 1804, Americans Lewis and Clark would begin their western expedition to the Pacific Ocean.

In 1800, French leader Napoléon Bonaparte pressured Spain to cede all of Louisiana to France. On October 1, 1800, the Treaty of San Ildefonso (an agreement between France and Spain) returned Louisiana to French ownership in exchange for a Spanish kingdom in Italy.[2] But Napoléon quickly realized that he did not have the resources to maintain the vast territory.

Napoléon reportedly told two of his ministers: "It is not only New Orleans that I will cede; it is the whole colony without my reservation."[3] In 1803, Napoléon sold Louisiana to the United States for $15 million in what was called the Louisiana Purchase. This greatly expanded the

territory of the United States. With that, France no longer held territory in the United States—only in Canada.

La Salle's Legacy

Some historians, like La Salle's contemporaries, have downplayed his achievements. They point to his poor people skills and his disastrous final expedition. Yet La Salle dared to dream big, and he had the commitment and courage to go after those dreams. The results were profound. As the introduction of the book *La Salle, the Mississippi, and the Gulf* stated: "Whatever assessment one may make of this strange and little-understood man—magnificent hero or blatant fool—at least one fact seems obvious: he influenced the geography and the history of North America as few have."[4]

Chapter 5

HIS LASTING IMPACT

In 1958, American poet Kenneth Rexroth wrote an essay about French influence in the United States. Though France had sold all of its territory in the present-day United States in 1803, "French life survived intact in hundreds of small isolated communities until well into the twentieth century," he wrote. "When I was a boy, during the First World War, I took a canoe trip down the Kankakee River from near Chicago to the Mississippi. We passed through many villages where hardly an inhabitant spoke a word of English."[1] Instead, the language that they spoke was French.

For more than three hundred years, French culture has flourished in parts of the United States. Much of this can be credited to the efforts of La Salle. When he arrived in North America in 1666, the middle of the continent was wide open for European settlement. It seemed that the Spanish, who had reached the Mississippi River back in 1541, might be the empire that would conquer the American heartland. But due largely to La Salle's claim of Louisiana, France controlled the middle third of the present-day United States from 1682 to 1763.

During that period, Indians may not have tolerated Spanish and British intrusion. But the French formed relatively good relations with many American Indians. One reason was that the French concentrated on the fur trade as opposed to farming. Thus, unlike the Spanish and British, they did not take over large sections of Indian land as settlements. The French hired American Indians as fur trappers, thereby establishing a different relationship with them.

In addition, the French made a strong effort to befriend the American Indians—La Salle in particular strived to do this. He spoke their languages, showered them with gifts and kindness, and even formed peace treaties among Indian tribes. Many Indians even went with him on his expeditions. Because of the friendliness of the French and particularly La Salle, New France was able to survive.

French Regions in America

As Kenneth Rexroth stated, a great deal of French culture has survived the centuries. Upper New England is home to a large French population, specifically in the states of Maine, Vermont, and New Hampshire. However, La Salle cannot take the credit for this. In the 1800s and early 1900s, many French-speaking Canadians moved to upper New England because of economic opportunities (construction, logging, the textile industry).

Besides New England, the United States's other French-heavy regions are between the Great Lakes and the Gulf of Mexico. This is where La Salle blazed his trails. Some places, in fact, were named after La Salle. They include La Salle, Illinois, along the Illinois River. In Chicago, the famous La Salle Street—which runs through the city's financial district—was named after him. Despite La Salle's failures in Texas, a county in south Texas was named after the explorer. Moreover, two cities in Canada honor this hero—La Salle, Ontario, and La Salle, Quebec. From 1927 to 1940, General Motors—based in Detroit, a former French settlement—produced the La Salle automobile, named after the explorer.

La Salle's Mississippi River voyage in 1682 took him past seven future U.S. states: Illinois, Missouri, Kentucky, Tennessee, Arkansas, Mississippi, and Louisiana. He was the first French explorer to make this trip. He built forts, and he claimed the territory for France. In subsequent years, the French pioneers who succeeded him established more forts and settlements in the region. French city names such as Louisville (Kentucky), Creve Coeur (Missouri), and D'Iberville (Mississippi), can be traced back to La Salle. Even Little Rock, the state capital of Arkansas, has a French origin. When French explorer Bernard de la Harpe arrived in the area in 1722, he called a

The French Quarter section of New Orleans still shows its French roots in its architecture. La Salle claimed the mouth of the Mississippi River near New Orleans as a possession of France.

small rock formation on the Arkansas River La Petite Roche, which translates to Little Rock.

🌐 LOUISIANA AND NEW ORLEANS

Of all the states, Louisiana has the strongest ties to La Salle. The state retains the name of the larger region that he called Louisiana. Moreover, when La Salle made the great proclamation of April 9, 1682, he was standing near present-day New Orleans, Louisiana.

In the late 1600s, French explorers, fur trappers, and traders arrived in that area. New Orleans (Nouvelle-Orléans in French) was officially founded in 1718 by Jean-Baptiste Le Moyne, Sieur de Bienville. As the gateway to the Mississippi River, an important trade route, the city grew rapidly. People from many cultures populated New Orleans, but the French influence was strong. Around 1800, large numbers of former Haitian slaves arrived in New Orleans. Haiti was a French colony in the Caribbean Sea, and the Haitian refugees spoke a language called Creole.

In 1836, New Orleans was divided into three sections. One of them was the French Quarter, which had been the center of town since the city's founding. Well into the 1800s, many descendents of the city's founders lived in the French Quarter and spoke the French language. In recent decades, the French Quarter has been one of America's

La Salle traveled all the way to the mouth of the Mississippi, where the river empties into the Gulf of Mexico. Pictured is a NASA image of the mouth of the Mississippi River.

most popular tourist destinations. Hurricane Katrina hit the area hard at the end of August 2005. However, the residents have started to rebuild, and tourists have begun to visit again.

The motto of New Orleans is *"Laissez les bon temps rouler"*—French for "Let the good times roll." That is not quite what La Salle had in mind for the area when he arrived in 1682. However, the city's strong French culture would undoubtedly make him proud.

Chapter 6

La Salle in the News

For many years, archaeologists in Texas contemplated the fate of the *Belle*, the last of La Salle's four ships. In 1686, violent weather had sunk the *Belle* near shore in the Matagorda Bay. Some optimists believed that they would find the ship's remains. After all, the bay is not very big, and its water is very shallow. In 1995, marine archaeologists searched for the shipwreck using a high-tech metal detector. On the very first day, they found it. All involved were ecstatic.

"This is tremendously exciting," said Barto Arnold, a marine archaeologist with the Texas Historical Commission. "It's a once-in-a-lifetime thing for an archaeologist to locate a site of this historical importance, this cultural importance."[1]

"No one expected the ship to be found," said Don Chipman, a history professor at the University of North Texas. "When you find a vessel like that with the cargo somewhat intact, it's kind of a time capsule that tells you a lot about the French who intended to colonize the area."[2]

With funding from the Texas State Historical Commission, workers hauled the ship and its contents to shore. The excavation lasted almost a year and produced more than a million artifacts. The objects included were three bronze cannons, thousands of glass beads, bronze bells, pottery, and coins. The settlers' possessions indicated that they had been serious about starting a large colony. They brought many trinkets that they likely intended to give as gifts to Indians.

However, the Karankawas harassed and killed many of the settlers, probably because of La Salle's disrespectful behavior toward them. Said La Salle biographer Robert S. Weddle, "He treated the Karankawas very high-handedly, and they didn't take kindly to it, according to some witnesses. They planned to destroy the colony almost from the moment of his arrival."[3]

The excavators found the skeleton of a crew member, whom they believe died of thirst. Next to the man's remains was a pewter cup with the inscription "C. Barange." On February 3, 2004, the sailor was buried in the Texas State Cemetery. As for the *Belle* artifacts, many of them are on display at the Bob Bullock Texas State History Museum.

Remarkably, the *Belle* was not the only La Salle-related discovery in recent years. Beginning in 1950, archaeologists began studying the area

The crew on a salvage ship takes a close look at a cannon from the *Belle*.

around La Salle's Fort St. Louis near Matagorda Bay. They found predominantly Spanish artifacts until 1996, when French cannons were excavated. Since then, archaeologists have unearthed the bones of French settlers as well as the remains of a building that the settlers constructed.

The Texas discoveries caused a buzz during the 1990s. But today, much farther north, another potential discovery continues to make news.

THE SEARCH FOR THE GRIFFON

Back in 1679, La Salle heard troubling news. The *Griffon*, the ship that his men had built and which was loaded with valuable furs, had disappeared in the northern Great Lakes. He himself attempted to look for the *Griffon* but could not find it. Over the course of three centuries, other adventurers attempted to hunt for the shipwreck, the oldest in the region. Said Scott Demel, curator at Chicago's Field Museum of Natural History, "I think everyone would agree it's the Holy Grail of the Great Lakes."[4]

Steven Libert, an amateur underwater explorer from Virginia, had been searching for the *Griffon* for more than twenty years. In 2001, he believed he found it. Libert was scuba diving in northern Lake Michigan, between Escanaba, Michigan, and the St. Martin Islands near Wisconsin. In the cold, deep water, he bumped into a long pole rising from the lake's bottom. "I didn't even know what it was," he said. "My face mask ran right into it. . . . Talk about shock."[5]

In 2002, Libert went back and videotaped his discovery with an infrared camera. He believed he found the *Griffon*'s bowsprit, a large pole that projects from the front of a ship. He thought the rest of the ship was buried below. Libert took Demel to the site to take samples of the pole.

Through carbon dating, they found that the ship had about a 33 percent chance of dating back to 1679.

Libert had other evidence suggesting that this could have been La Salle's ship. Marks on the wood indicated that the boat was built with axes—just as the *Griffon* was. In addition, Libert wrote, "the measured distance between each trunnel [tree nail] (center to center) measures 12.8 inches, exactly the French foot 'pied.'" In addition, he wrote, "The location is consistent with Father Louis Hennepin's diary."[6]

Though Libert discovered the ship, he struggled to obtain the rights to salvage it. He had to battle in the courts with the state of Michigan, which claims all rights to shipwrecks within its waters. To help his cause, Libert turned to the French government because the *Griffon* had sailed under the French flag. Libert convinced the French to claim the ship as its own and to give him salvage rights.

In December 2006, Libert lost a court case against Michigan. But a month later, he filed an appeal. As Libert wrote, "In the words of John Paul Jones, 'I (WE) have not yet begun to fight.' Our fight is with the state of Michigan, not the country of France, as France is the sovereign and sole owner of this vessel!"[7] In April 2008, a federal appeals court ruled that the federal government has authority over the shipwreck until the dispute over ownership and salvage rights is resolved.

Meanwhile, a ship still lies in the cold, dark waters of Lake Michigan. Is it really the *Griffon*, the first ship known to sail the Great Lakes? Historians would love to know. If he were still with us, so would La Salle.

Chapter Notes

Chapter 1. Dreams of Adventure

1. Andrew Santella, *Sieur de La Salle* (Chicago: Reed Educational & Professional Publishing, 2002), p. 6.

Chapter 2. The First Explorations

1. Donald S. Johnson, *La Salle: A Perilous Odyssey from Canada to the Gulf of Mexico* (New York: Cooper Square Press, 2002), p. 28.

2. Francis Parkman and Samuel Eliot Morison, *The Francis Parkman Reader* (Canada: De Capo Press, 1998), pp. 198–199.

3. Francis Parkman, *The Discovery of the Great West* (Boston: Little, Brown, and Company, 1870), p. 8.

4. Francis Parkman, *La Salle and the Discovery of the Great West* (Boston: Little, Brown, and Company; Chicago and St. Louis: E. Holdoway and Company, 1897), p. 120.

Chapter 3. Down the Mighty Mississippi

1. Donald S. Johnson, *La Salle: A Perilous Odyssey from Canada to the Gulf of Mexico* (New York: Cooper Square Press, 2002), p. 104.

2. Ibid., p. 109.

3. Henry James Morgan, *Sketches of Celebrated Canadians* (London, Rose & Co., 1862), p. 23.

4. Ibid.

5. Johnson, p. 111.

6. Ibid., p. 112.

7. Ibid., p. 120.

8. Francis Parkman, *France and England in North America*, Volume 1 (New York: Library of America, 1983), pp. 965–966.

9. John Reynolds, *The Pioneer History of Illinois* (Chicago: Fergus Printing Company, 1887), p. 39.

10. Dan Parker, "Raising the Belle," Corpus Christi Caller Times, 1996, <www.coastalbendhealth.com/newsarch/lasalle1.htm> (April 8, 2007).

Chapter 4. La Salle's Historical Importance

1. The History of Warren County Ohio, *Warren County OHGenWeb Site*, November 3, 2004, <http://www.rootsweb.com/~ohwarren/Beers/I/0032.htm> (April 17, 2007).

2. Louisiana Purchase, *The Lewis and Clark Journey of Discovery*, n.d., <http://www.nps.gov/archive/jeff/LewisClark2/Circa1804/Heritage/LouisianaPurchase/LouisianaPurchase.htm> (May 9, 2008).

3. "Chicago Day," *Omaha Public Library*, 1998, <http://www.omaha.lib.ne.us/transmiss/secretary/chicagoday.html> (April 19, 2007).

4. Robert S. Weddle, ed. *La Salle, Mississippi, and the Gulf* (College Station: Texas A&M University Press, 1987), p. 11.

Chapter 5. His Lasting Impact

1. Kenneth Rexroth, "The Influence of French Poetry on American," *Bureau of Public Secrets*, n.d., <http://www.bopsecrets.org/rexroth/essays/frenchpoetry.htm> (April 24, 2007).

Chapter 6. La Salle in the News

1. Associated Press, "Sunken cannon may be La Salle's," Corpus *Christi Caller Times*, July 14, 1995, <http://www.coastalbendhealth.com/newsarch/lasalle3.htm> (April 9, 2007).

2. Dan Parker, "Raising the Belle," *Corpus Christi Caller Times*, 1996, <www.coastalbendhealth.com/newsarch/lasalle1.htm> (April 8, 2007).

3. Ibid.

4. Peggy Walsh-Sarnecki, "Mystery of the Griffon: Search for Great Lakes oldest shipwreck," *Cyber Diver News Network*, January 2, 2006, <http://www.cdnn.info/news/industry/i060102.html> (April 10, 2007).

5. Ibid.

6. Author email interview, May 7, 2007.

7. Steve Libert, "Re: The Griffon," *Great Lakes Shipwreck Research Group*, January 18, 2007, <http://www.shipwreck.com/wreckboard/> (April 22, 2007).

Glossary

archaeologist—A professional who searches for and studies material evidence from past human life and culture.

armorer—One who manufactures and repairs arms (weapons) and armor.

astronomy—The scientific study of the universe outside the Earth's atmosphere.

basin—An area that is drained by a river and its tributaries.

blasphemy—The act of insulting or showing contempt for God.

bluff—A high, steep bank, often overlooking a body of water.

confederacy—A union of persons, parties, or states that is formed for mutual support or common action.

conspirator—One who engages in a secret agreement with others to commit an unlawful act.

creditor—A person or business to whom one owes money.

deserter—A person who abandons his or her duty or group.

marshland—Wet land with grassy vegetation, usually located near water.

minister— A high-ranking government official who heads a ministry or department.

missionary—Someone who tries to convert others to his or her religion.

navigation—The science of directing or plotting the course of a vessel.

New France—North American territory colonized by France (1534–1763).

New World—What Europeans in the sixteenth and seventeenth centuries called the Americas and the islands in the Caribbean.

raze—Destroy; tear down.

salvage—Rescue the remains of a shipwreck.

settlement—A community of people who settle far from home but maintain ties to their homeland.

square—An open area where multiple streets meet and where people tend to gather.

tributary—A river or stream that flows into a larger river or stream.

zealot—One who is strongly, perhaps overly, passionate about a cause.

Further Reading

Bruseth, James E. and Toni S. Hunter. *From a Watery Grave: The Discovery and Excavation of La Salle's Shipwreck, La Belle.* College Station: Texas A&M University Press, 2005.

Faber, Harold. *La Salle: Down the Mississippi.* New York: Benchmark Books, 2002.

Goodman, Joan Elizabeth. *Despite All Obstacles: La Salle and the Conquest of the Mississippi.* New York: Mikaya Press, 2001.

Mitchell, Mark G. *Raising La Belle.* Austin, Tex.: Eakin Press, 2002.

Snider, Janet and Betty Sherwood. *La Salle and the Rise of New France.* Toronto: Canchron Books, 2005.

Zronik, John. *Sieur de La Salle: New World Adventurer.* New York: Crabtree Pub. Co., 2006.

INTERNET ADDRESSES

La Salle
<http://library.thinkquest.org/J002678F/la_salle.htm>

NOVA Online—Voyage of Doom
<http://www.pbs.org/wgbh/nova/lasalle/>

Pathfinders & Passageways—The Exploration of Canada: "Cavelier De La Salle Pushes the Boundaries of New France"
<http://www.collectionscanada.gc.ca/2/24/h24-1480-e.html>

Index